Nicole

Maria Montessori

a biography for and by children

Alison Ney, Linda Seeley, Cameron Sesto

& The Children's House Students
of Stoneridge Children's Montessori School

MᶜM

Master Class Materials

"I beg the dear all powerful children to unite with me for the building of peace in man."~ gravestone quote, Maria Montessori

Alison Ney — *Author, Montessori Teacher*
Linda Seeley — *Montessori Teacher and Teacher Trainer*
Cameron Sesto — *Design, Production, Montessori Art Teacher*
Children's House Students at Stoneridge Montessori School — *Illustrations*

Dedicated to the memory of Maria Montessori
and her love of children

Dr. Montessori was born in Italy.

Long, long ago, on August
31st in the year 1870,
a baby girl was born in
Chiaravalle, Italy.

Italy is a country shaped
like a boot in the continent
of Europe.

Mr. and Mrs Montessori named their daughter Maria.

The baby's parents named her Maria. Her mother's name was Renilde and her father's name was Alessandro.

Oh, how they loved their baby, Maria!

Di Montessori first
wanted
to be an
engineer

Maria thought she might like to be an engineer when she grew up. But Maria's father told her that girls could absolutely NOT be engineers.

Maria's mother disagreed. She told Maria that she could be ANYTHING she wanted to be.

Dr Montessori was
the first doctor
in Italy

So Maria went to technical school. She learned so much! While she was there, Maria decided that she would like to be a doctor instead.

Once again, Maria's father said, "No!" But Maria's mother thought she could be a wonderful doctor.

I love how she was the first doctor in Italy

Maria's father was not happy with her decision to enter medical school; nevertheless, he walked her to class every day.

Maria studied hard and even had to work alone in her classroom at night. She learned to be a doctor.

Maria graduated at the top of her class and became one of the first female doctors in Italy!

Dr Montessori became a teacher because she loved children

As a doctor, Maria started to work with children. She saw that they could do so many things that nobody thought they could do.

Dr. Montessori made us materials like the buoad prisns and pink Tower.

Maria began to make materials like the pink tower, the red rods, cylinder blocks, and many other learning tools that we have in Montessori schools right now.

Dr. Montessori started a school
called the Casa dei Bambini.

Maria decided that she should start a school. This time her mother and father were both supportive. She started a small school in Rome called the Casa dei Bambini. That means "Children's House" in Italian.

Dr. Montessori na-med her school The casa dei Bambini

The children in Maria's school learned to cook and to take care of each other, their classroom, and Mother Earth. People began to notice Maria's little school. They saw children reading, writing, caring for one another, and being polite. They wondered how Maria was able to guide so many children in this way.

Dr. Montesori made materialsfor us.

Maria began to write books describing her lessons and materials.

One of her first books was called **The Montessori Method**. People came to visit the Casa dei Bambini from all over the world.

Maria started to travel and to teach people about Montessori schools.

Or maria had a baby named Mario

During this time, Maria had her own little baby. She called him Mario.

Maria kept traveling the world. She trained teachers, taught children, and wrote more books about her work.

Dr Montessori had a baby boy named Mario.

When Mario grew up he began to travel with his mother. He went with her to India and many other interesting places.

Maria Montessori
was a peacemaker
because she loved children.

One of the most important things Maria taught children was how to be peaceful.

Maria Montessori was
nominated for the Nobel
Peace Prize.

Dr. Montessori became known as a citizen of the world and was admired and respected by the leaders of many countries including the Queen of England and Mahatma Gandhi.

She was even nominated for the Nobel Peace Prize three times! She knew that children could help adults learn to live in peace and harmony.

When Maria was older, she went to live in Holland. She especially liked being there because the people loved and respected children so much.

Dr Montessori wanted the whole world to be peaceful.

She knew children could change the world. She wrote a book called **Education and Peace** in which she described her plan to help the world live in peace. She felt that this was her most important book.

Maria Montessori died in 1952 in her garden in Holland

She was 81 years old when she died peacefully in her garden in Holland.

Dr. Montessori started schools all over the world.

At the time she died, Maria was planning a trip to help start schools in Ghana, a country in Africa.

Dr Montessori was a
doctor and a teacher

We remember Maria Montessori for all of the work she did to teach us how to be peaceful, caring and respectful toward one another and toward the Earth.

Maria Montessori: Her Life and Work

1870 Born in Chiaravalle, Italy, August 31.

1880 Becomes very ill and nearly dies.

1882 Parents try to encourage her to become a teacher. Montessori becomes interested mathematics and engineering.

1886 Montessori attends technical school. (Later she becomes interested in biology and the field of medicine.)

1896 Montessori becomes one of the first women doctors to graduate from the University of Rome Medical School.

She joins the staff of the University Psychiatric Clinic, where she works with children with intellectual disabilities. She begins to study the works of Jean Marc Gaspard Itard and Edouard Séguin.

1898 Named Director of the State Orthophrenic Institute.

Works again with children with intellectual disabilities for two years.

Her baby Mario is born.

Lectures at pedagogical conferences.

1900 Returns to the University of Rome to study philosophy, psychology, and anthropology.

Becomes Lecturer of Anthropology and Hygiene at the Royal Feminine Teacher Training College in Rome.

1904 Appointed Lecturer of Anthropology at the Royal University of Rome, a post she keeps until 1916.

1900–1907

Practices medicine in clinics, hospitals, and in her own private practice.

Continues to lecture at the University of Rome.

1907 The first *Casa dei Bambini* in the slums of San Lorenzo Italy, January 6.

Second *Casa dei Bambini* opens in San Lorenzo, on April 7th.

1908 A *Casa dei Bambini* opens in Milan, where Anna Maccheroni developed the music materials.

1909 All of Italian Switzerland begins using the Montessori Method in their orphanages and kindergartens.

1910 Another *Casa dei Bambini* opens in Barcelona, where spiritual teaching is developed.

1912 Montessori makes her first visit to the United States.
The American Montessori Association is formed.

1913 Montessori returns to Europe.

1915 Montessori returns to the United States.
First Montessori course starts in the United States in California.
Montessori class set up at San Francisco World's Fair. It wins two gold medals for education.

1916 Montessori travels for a year between the United States and Spain giving courses and lectures.

1919 First international course established in England.

1922 Montessori appointed Government Inspector of Schools in Italy.

1923 Presented a Doctorate of Letters, December 11 for her work as an expert in the field of psychiatry, medicine and anthropology.

1927 Montessori Society of Argentina is formed.

1929 The formation of Association Montessori Internationale (AMI).

1936 Montessori establishes permanent residence in the Netherlands.

1939 Montessori travels to India to give the first Indian course.
Establishes the first age 6-12 course with her son, Mario.

1949 Montessori is nominated for the Nobel Peace Prize (also in 1950 & 1951).

1952 Dr. Maria Montessori dies May 6, and is buried in Holland.

1957 American renaissance for Montessori education begins.

1964 Montessori Head Start Programs begin in the United States.

1965 People of Chiaravalle dedicate a plaque to honor Montessori and her work.

1968 The beginning of public Montessori Schools in the United States.

1978 The development of *Erdkinder* (ages 12-18) programs in the United States.

If you already work in a Montessori environment, we hope this presentation of the life and work of Maria Montessori has reinforced your commitment to the work she started at the first Casa dei Bambini. If you are new to the Montessori world, we hope you are inspired to learn more about her philosophy and methods. To help you share this story with your children, we suggest two follow up activities.

The first is creating an object box that includes important items from the story of Maria Montessori's life. These objects include dolls to represent the people in the story, a flag of Italy, a small globe, a peace postcard, a small model of the Casa dei Bambini and other toy items that reflect the life of Maria. These concrete objects will help children remember and retell the story of her life and the development of her work.

The second activity involves paper dolls that children can cut out and decorate to represent Maria and her family. Templates of these dolls are available on our website at **www.masterclassmaterials.com.** On the site, you will also find more information about the object box, including pictures of children using it in the classroom.

The End

Made in the USA
Middletown, DE
21 June 2016